Old DUNFERMLINE

by
William F. Hendrie

To Jim and Linda Brown, whose collection of pictures, enthusiasm and knowledge and love of Dunfermline helped bring about this book.

An unidentified group of behatted ladies aboard an open-topped Dunfermline & District Tramways car.
On the side is an advertisement for the Dunfermline Opera House.

© William F. Hendrie 2002
First published in the United Kingdom, 2002,
reprinted 2005, 2009
by Stenlake Publishing Ltd.
01290 551122
www.stenlake.co.uk

ISBN 9781840331943
**The publishers regret that they cannot supply copies
of any pictures featured in this book.**

The publishers would like to thank Robert Grieves for providing
additional information about motor transport in this book.

INTRODUCTION

The King sits in Dunfermling toune drynking the bluid-red wyne

These opening lines from the Ballad of Sir Patrick Spens, which generations of Scottish school pupils committed to memory, act as an apt reminder that in the Middle Ages Dunfermline was frequently visited by Scottish monarchs on their regular, royal progresses through their domain. Most famously it was there that Princess Margaret sought out King Malcolm III, Malcolm Canmore, when she was shipwrecked on the shores of the River Forth in 1069 following the Norman Conquest of England. Having found the king in royal residence at the palace (whose ruins are still a prominent landmark in Dunfermline over 900 years later) Margaret succeeded in captivating him to such an extent that she soon became his second wife. As Queen Margaret she used her influence to convert Scotland to Roman Catholicism and introduced the famous Queen's Ferry across the Forth to encourage pilgrims to come to worship at the holy shrine which she established in Dunfermline, along with a Benedictine priory.

It was her third son, David I, who upgraded the priory and founded Dunfermline Abbey, whose magnificent massive-pillared Norman nave still adjoins the town's Gothic-revival style parish church. Around the parapet of the church tower the words 'King Robert The Bruce' are carved in large letters for all to see, in proud recognition of the fact that it is within its walls that the body of the victor of Bannockburn lies buried.

Almost two centuries later Dunfermline's royal importance was strengthened still further when King James VI of Scotland and I of England chose to expand the Abbey guest house into a royal residence for his young bride, Princess Anne of Denmark. It was there that she gave birth to the future King Charles I, the last British monarch to be born in Scotland. Dunfermline gained the status of a royal burgh in the late sixteenth century, and the pattern of its medieval streets can still be traced.

The removal of the Scottish court to London in 1603 led to a reduction in Dunfermline's importance, but by the early eighteenth century its prosperity had begun to increase again thanks to the growth of the weaving trade. At first this was developed on a domestic basis by handloom workers in their cottage homes, but 100 years later the introduction of power looms led to the town being caught up in the Industrial Revolution. Dunfermline rapidly expanded to become the world's leading centre for the production of damask linen cloth, and along with its coal-mining activities this led to it becoming an important hub which to this day dominates the whole of West Fife.

With all of this activity it was perverse that the family of Dunfermline's most famous son, Andrew Carnegie, was forced to emigrate to America to find work. Carnegie, however, never forgot this 'romantic town', as he later described it, and when he returned to Scotland having made his fortune it was here that he lavished his greatest gifts, bringing some sweetness and light into the lives of the town's toiling masses. As a result of his generosity Dunfermline is blessed with an impressive array of public facilities including the Carnegie Centre, the Carnegie Hall, the Carnegie Library and perhaps most importantly of all Pittencrieff Glen, considered by many to be Scotland's finest public park.

In the twentieth century Dunfermline's importance was increased still further by the British government's decision to establish Scotland's only Royal Naval Dockyard near it at Rosyth on the River Forth. The dockyard has now been converted to civilian use and has been chosen as the terminal for the new direct passenger ferry link with the continent. This new service will ensure that many more European visitors will soon be following in the wake of that wily skipper, Sir Patrick Spens, to discover Dunfermling toune.

Opposite: The first motorbuses in Fife were registered in Dunfermline on 23 June 1909, the same year that the trams which they were to replace totally within three decades were introduced to the town. On that day the first of the three vehicles to be registered was a fifteen-seat Arrol-Johnston owned by George Scott from Culross. The other two both also belonged to a Culross owner, Tom Cousin: they were a fifteen-seat Halley and a ten-seat Albion. A three-times daily service between Culross and Dunfermline was soon established with the buses arriving and departing from a stance in Chalmers Street. The Leyland PLSC3 bus in the picture, registration number FG 3951, was bought new by Simpson's Motor Service of Market Street, Dunfermline in 1928. This photograph was taken at the Abbey gates when it was on the Dunfermline to Inverkeithing service. Frank Simpson started as a driver with Cousin's Bus Service of Culross before purchasing his own bus in 1923 which he operated between Dunfermline and Inverkeithing. Rapid expansion of routes soon followed with the introduction of many services throughout West Fife and one all the way to Glasgow. Simpson's company was acquired by Walter Alexander in 1929 who joined forces with A. & R. Forrester of Lochgelly the same year. The Simpson & Forrester buses continued, however, to run under that name until 1938 when they were absorbed into Alexander's Bluebird fleet.

Trams were introduced to the town in November 1909 by the Dunfermline & District Tramway Company. The track (which had a gauge of 3' 6") was brought to the town by ship from Middlesborough via the harbour at Charlestown, but before it could be laid the level of Townhill Road had to be lowered to provide enough clearance for trams to pass below the railway bridge which carried main line trains to the Upper station. Granite setts for the trackbed were imported from Norway. The first 20 trams were brought to Dunfermline by rail and were all of the open top double deck kind seen in this photograph, taken at the terminus at East Port.

Although their top decks were open to the elements, the trams provided an efficient means of transport and were able to reach speeds of up to 16 m.p.h. on the open stretches of track, which was a big improvement on previous methods of transport. It was soon possible to travel all the way to Cowdenbeath via Halbeath and Crossgates, with the track reaching Lochgelly on 23 December 1909. Kelty was added to the list of destinations in 1910, but the long-awaited track from Townhill to Rumbling Bridge via the High Street was not completed until 1913. The final expansion of the Dunfermline & District tramway system came in 1918 when a track to Rosyth was completed, transporting workers to and from the newly-established Royal Naval Dockyard. Despite their popularity, the days of the trams were comparatively short-lived and in 1937 it was decided to replace them with buses, which could provide more flexible services. The final tram departed on Sunday 10 July 1937, a day chosen because it was reckoned that it would be the quietest day of the year because of local holidays. On the following morning Alexander & Sons Bluebird buses took over the routes. Within days there were protests about poorer service and higher fares, but these came too late as the trams had already been taken to Hill of Beath to be scrapped. This view shows one of the trams at the terminus at East Port, with the spire of the Sheriff Court rising behind it. Dick's Co-operative Institute, with its distinctive frontage, can be seen on the right behind the tram.

A lone passenger takes in the view from the open top deck of tram No. 11 as it makes its way along Chalmers Street past the junction with Pittencrieff Street en route to Lochore. The only other traffic in sight is a horse-drawn cart making its morning milk round. The milk was contained in the large churns seen on the back of the cart and housewives wishing to purchase pints had to bring out their own jugs in which to collect the milk. In the foreground on the left a gents' hairdressers advertises its presence with a traditional red and white striped pole. This was originally the sign in the Middle Ages for the barber-surgeons of the period. The red stripes represented their prowess at blood letting, a primitive practice which was supposed to improve patients' health, and the white stripes signified the bandages with which they staunched the flow. Many of the buildings on the right were later demolished to make way for the Glen Bridge which was completed in 1932. The spire of the North Parish Church can be glimpsed behind the tram; adjacent to it were the premises of the American Consulate in Dunfermline. Apart from Edinburgh, Glasgow and Dundee, Dunfermline and Kirkcaldy were the only towns in Scotland with their own American Consulates. They remained until the close of the 1930s, partly to serve the large number of Fife families who used them to obtain the necessary visas to enable them to begin new lives in the USA.

The single tram track that ran along the length of the High Street doubled as the street opened out into East Port. The boy stepping onto the pavement at the left of the picture is wearing a uniform, complete with pillbox hat, which may be that of the Boys Brigade, a popular youth organisation in the town during the nineteenth and twentieth centuries. The opening beside the advertising billboards on the right is the top of the New Row – for many years policemen and traffic wardens directed the traffic at this busy junction. The white awnings at the tram stop were shielding the windows of John Ross & Co.'s umbrella, luggage and saddlery store at 6 East Port. It also supplied thousands of leather satchels in which generations of Dunfermline bairns carried their schoolbooks, jotters and play pieces on their backs to school.

This early view looking down the length of the High Street from the Cross shows its cobbled surface before the tram tracks were laid in 1913. Despite its antiquity, the scene is still a familiar one with the imposing tower of the City Chambers looming in the background. The building in the foreground with the distinctive crow-stepped gable still stands. Although it is no longer the publishing office of the *Dunfermline Press*, this popular local newspaper is still in existence, and as well as serving local readers many copies are sent overseas to keep exiled natives up to date with local developments. A whole range of picture postcards can be seen in the newspaper office window. In the days before most townsfolk possessed telephones, postcards were the usual way of sending messages. As there was an afternoon mail delivery a card posted first thing in the morning could be used to confirm attendance at a function that evening, or even to say that you were going to be late home for tea! Notice too the single gas lamp on the corner which was the sole means of illuminating this busy crossing after dark.

Looking in the opposite direction to the previous view, this picture of the High Street was taken several years later. Several of the shops visible here had a High Street presence for many decades, including Tyler's boot and shoe shop on the right and Lipton's the grocers opposite, famous for its teas. Next door to Lipton's was A. & D. Hoey's drapery store, to which many Dunfermline children made annual pilgrimages towards the end of the summer holidays to be fitted with school uniforms for the start of the new term. In the background the tall spire of the Guildhall rises above the other buildings. This was built in 1808 as part of an attempt to have Dunfermline recognised as Fife's county town. This proved unsuccessful, and in 1820 the building was converted into a hotel, later becoming the sheriff court. It served this purpose until 1963 when the court moved to Carnegie Drive, and the Guildhall now serves as the local job centre.

The famous store of F. W. Woolworth first came to Dunfermline in 1922 and traded from this shop for many years before building larger premises on the opposite side of the High Street (seen in the picture opposite). Unlike in the previous two pictures, motor cars are present here, but at this stage were so few in number that parking in the High Street still presented no problems. The French–Gothic style City Chambers building was opened without ceremony in 1879, having taken four years to construct. It was designed by Edinburgh architect Mr J. C. Walker and cost approximately £20,000. The tower is 23 feet square and 117 feet high; the spire was a later addition. In the background the newly-installed Louise Carnegie Gates can be glimpsed at the main entrance to Pittencrieff Glen.

The High Street was bustling with pedestrians but strangely clear of traffic when this later postcard view was produced. The photographer may have deliberately chosen a time when no vehicles were in sight because the inclusion of cars in a shot could easily date a card, thus reducing the period during which it could be sold as a modern view. Well-known businesses which can be seen in this picture include Hepworths men's outfitters on the left and Smith's pork butchers. The latter was owned by a family of German immigrants called Schmidt, who like many other such immigrants in Scottish towns chose to anglicise their name as a result, no doubt, of anti-German feeling during the war and inter-war years. On the same side of the street as Hepworths, and advertised by its signage at roof level (visible more clearly in the picture on page 8), is the City Restaurant. Bruce's Cafe on the first floor was a favourite meeting place for morning coffee, lunch and afternoon tea, and was especially well-known for its high teas.

This photograph of the High Street was taken after World War II. The AA sign at second floor level on the right indicates the premises of the Inglis Royal Hotel. Further along on the same side of the street was the 1,875 seat Regal Cinema, which opened in 1931 on the site of the earlier Olympia Picture House. The Regal showed its final film on 29 May 1976. Next door was another of the High Street's best-loved attractions, Maloco's Cafe, where many young people met their friends, while down the narrow lane to the side of it was the Maloco family's equally famous Empire Billiard Saloon with its sixteen tables.

There was drama in the High Street one Saturday afternoon in 1904 when this nine-ton girder made by the Dalziel Bridge & Roof Building Co. of Motherwell came to grief, crashing through the windows of the London & Newcastle Tea Co.'s shop, next door to Tyler's boot and shoe shop. At the time of the accident it was being transported along the High Street on two bogies pulled by a steam traction engine. The girder was due to become part of a bridge on the Dunfermline to Alloa and Stirling railway line, and the problem of how to move the monster load was a difficult one to solve. In the end it was decided to abandon its journey by road and instead to transport it slowly to Dunfermline Upper station for onward transportation by rail. The next morning the High Street was closed and the slow business of recovering the girder began. In the end it took eleven hours to carefully manoeuvre it to the railway station. The premises to the left are those of W. Clark & Son, printers. A large thermometer advertising Stephen's ink is attached to their outside wall.

The proprietors of the new Cinema Picture House in East Port were apparently not superstitious, choosing to screen their first film on 13 September 1913. The grand opening was presided over by manager David Longmuir and the *Dunfermline Press* in its next edition reported that the cinema had been filled to capacity. Talkies were first shown on 15 August 1931, and throughout the 1930s and the years of World War II queues of patrons waiting patiently for admittance often stretched into the High Street. The coming of television in the early 1950s, however, caused a drastic reduction in audiences and the cinema closed on 8 August 1959. Just six weeks later, on 26 September, it was bought by Caledonian Associated Cinemas of Inverness. They decided to rebuild the premises as

only the second new cinema to be built in Scotland since World War II, and it thus began a new lease of life on 2 January 1965 with the film *Fifty Five Days in Peking* starring Charlton Heston and Ava Gardner. In 1982 it was renamed the Orient Express and was divided up to provide three screens, but cinema audiences again declined and despite efforts in 1992 by Robin Cinemas (a small independent London operator) to keep it open, this East Port place of entertainment finally closed. Other popular former Dunfermline cinemas included the Regal, Alhambra and Kinema. Now that cinema-going is again a popular pastime, Dunfermline film enthusiasts are served by a new multi-screen cinema complex which has been established near Halbeath, where the M90 motorway provides audiences with ready access.

This peaceful scene shows Kirkgate with the tower of Dunfermline Abbey in the background. Maygate can be seen leading off to the left. The word 'gate' in these place names comes not from an archway, but from the old Scottish word 'gait' meaning stride, and its use in this fashion is also found in many Scandinavian cities. Dunfermline police station was for many years situated where the car is seen parked on the right-hand side of the street and the cells there remained in use until the mid 1970s. Fraser & Carmichael wholesale grocers occupied the building on the corner on the left.

The Abbott House, Dunfermline.   *Christie.*

Abbot House is now the home of Dunfermline's Heritage Centre and is open to visitors every day of the year apart from Christmas Day and New Year's Day. It is known as the Pink House because of the attractive colour wash used to restore its ancient harled walls to their original condition. Until the Reformation in 1560, Abbot House was the home of the chief monk at the adjacent Abbey and was one of the principal buildings in the complex which made up the domestic quarters of the town's monastery. After the decline of the Catholic Church it was used for several different purposes including a privately-owned mansion, an iron foundry and an art college. It has now been beautifully restored and contains displays relating to the town's history from the Middle Ages to more recent times. There is also a souvenir shop and a cafe offering home baking, which on summer days can be enjoyed at tables in the gardens with their fragrant-smelling herb beds which have also been recreated.

Dunfermline Co-operative Society was founded in 1851 with its first shop in South Chapel Street (later renamed Randolph Street). It proved a highly successful business, despite the destruction of its Randolph Street premises by this disastrous fire in February 1923. Over £50,000 worth of damage was done, but the Co-op continued to flourish and later moved its headquarters to a three-storey department store in the High Street. As well as its many shops in the town centre and its branch stores in the surrounding areas, the Co-op also operated many delivery rounds. To begin with these were made by a fleet of horse-drawn carts and later vans which delivered everything from milk, morning rolls and bran scones before breakfast through to butcher meat and groceries. In the afternoons the bakery vans did their rounds offering a whole range of tea breads and cakes to serve at afternoon and high teas.

Members of the Co-op board showed what forward-looking businessmen they were in 1916 by being amongst the first in Dunfermline to place an order for motor vehicles, in this case two Ford vans, although it was many decades before the last horse finally departed from the Co-op stables. The Co-op, or the 'store' as it was often known, was far more than just a place to shop. With its membership scheme, its mutual savings scheme and its famous quarterly dividend, it was much more a way of life, with many Dunfermline people depending on it to provide everything from their babies' prams and nappies right through to funeral services.

Apart from the Co-op and chain stores such as Woolworths, the Danish Dairy and Lipton's, Dunfermline has also had many enterprising local shop owners, one of whom was Miss Beveridge. She ran her busy newsagents and tobacconists business for many years at 19 Campbell Street, outside which placards advertised the latest issues of the *Daily Record*, published in Glasgow and the *Courier*, printed every morning in Dundee. On the day this photograph was taken news of relief for local unemployed miners and a storm at sea which had resulted in the loss of 25 lives were making the headlines. As in the picture of the former newspaper office at the Cross (page 8), note the range of local picture postcards. These are displayed in front of the big bottles of boilings and other sweets which were also sold by Miss Beveridge.

This tobacconists and newsagents shop in East Port was run by Mr J. M. Bryce. Much of his trade came from passengers waiting to board trams at the nearby terminus, while in the evening he stayed open late to sell chocolate, sweets and cigarettes to people going to the continuous shows at the Cinema Picture House in the days long before a ban on smoking in cinemas was considered. The tall board to the left of the shop window advertises the *Scotsman*, the *Daily Record* and the *Courier*, while the one on the right promotes the latest children's comics including the *Marvel*, the *Gem* and *Chips*. Listed in addition to these popular boys' weeklies are the now-forgotten *Forget Me Not* and *Pansy Library*, which presumably provided weekly reading for girls such as the wee lassie standing beside Mr Bryce in this picture.

A tall mill chimney looms behind this corner shop at the junction of Gardeners Street and Townhill Road. There is no smoke coming from the factory lum, but smokes galore are advertised in the shop windows and a prominent Gold Flake cigarette sign adorns the wall at a time before the dangers of tobacco were widely recognised.

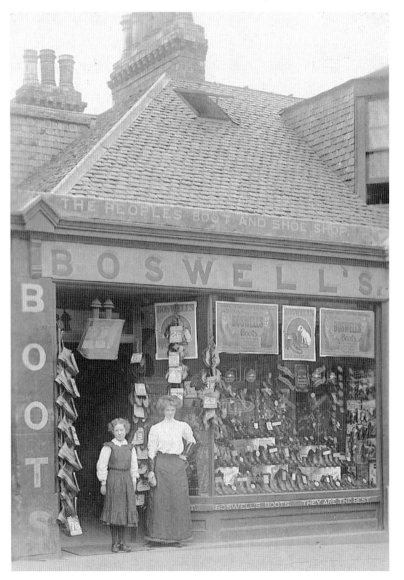

Boswell's Wholesale and Retail Boot and Shoe Manufacturer was a locally-owned rival to the nationwide chain of Tyler's boot and shoe shops. With its main branch at 45 High Street, Boswell's sold not only footwear but a wide range of leggings and gaiters, the latter guaranteed to keep feet dry from splashes from muddy puddles and even downpours of rain. Amongst the range of men's shoes advertised in the window of this branch are its popular Balmoral Boots, which sold at five shillings and sixpence. Boswell's also had branches in Alloa and Dundee. It is not clear whether both the ladies standing in the doorway are shop assistants, or whether the younger one is a school-aged daughter who has stopped to call on her mother on her way home. It was obviously a warm day, as both the window and the skylight are wide open.

The stone-walled, slate-roofed premises of Pittencrieff Primary School still stand in Dewar Street, near the north-west entrance to Pittencrieff Glen. Its tall, narrow windows were specifically designed to allow ample light into the classrooms without giving pupils the opportunity to waste valuable time by staring out of them. A former pupil recalls that latecomers were automatically punished with painful palmies – strokes on the hand with the headmaster's long, leather tawse – which he could certainly draw! He adds, 'When I was older it added insult to injury to know that the straps with which we were belted regularly were nicknamed Lochgellies, because they were made only a few miles away in the neighbouring mining village by John Dick, the saddler.' The thickest tawse, often with three, instead of the usual two thongs, were known as Lochgelly Specials. Their ability to inflict instant stinging discomfort without causing any lasting injury meant that as well as being used by local teachers and others all over Scotland, they were in demand from schools throughout the British Empire. In 1912 boys from Commercial School (also in Dunfermline) staged a strike both for shorter school days and to object against the number of strappings to which they alleged they were subjected – not only for misbehaviour, but also for mistakes in their work. Their protests were unsuccessful, however.

Pittencrieff School Dunfermline

Despite the strictness of discipline in local schools, many former Dunfermline pupils still have fond memories of their schooldays, especially those spent at the High School and the Lauder Technical Institute, whose premises were originally adjacent to each other, as seen here. The substantial three-storey premises of the High School, topped by a lofty belfry and an ornate cupola, were opened in 1886. They were occupied by the school's pupils until the current premises were opened at St Leonard's in 1939. The Lauder Technical Institute (familiarly known as the 'Grey Tech' to distinguish it from another Dunfermline building called the 'Red Tech' and built of pink sandstone from Dumfriesshire) was yet another of Andrew Carnegie's gifts to his home town. Carnegie chose to name the technical institute in honour of his uncle, George Lauder, who had been prominent in radical politics in the town and who he very much admired. Dunfermline's further education college now occupies spacious modern premises on the east side of the town, but still proudly bears the name of Lauder College.

The welfare of women was high on Andrew Carnegie's agenda when he gifted Dunfermline its imposing four-storey Women's Institute in Pilmuir Street, which was opened by Mrs Carnegie in 1912. The building was later bought by the Reo Stakis organisation and converted into the Belleville Hotel and Stakis Steak House. When it closed in 1982 the premises reopened as Johnston's bar, club and entertainment centre and now house an amusement arcade.

Women's Institute, Dunfermline

Carnegie Baths, Dunfermline

The fine premises of the Carnegie Baths in Pilmuir Street are still in busy daily use as the Carnegie Leisure Centre. Andrew Carnegie first gifted public baths to Dunfermline in 1877, several years before either Edinburgh or Glasgow had such facilities. They were replaced by those in the building pictured here, whose foundation stone was laid by Mrs Louise Carnegie on 5 July 1902 and whose premises, which also contained Turkish baths, a spacious gymnasium and a billiard hall, were officially opened in 1905. All of these facilities are still in use, with the original pool used mainly for swimming lessons and training sessions, while a new modern pool has been built next door for leisure use.

THE SWIMMING POND, DUNFERMLINE.

The appearance of Carnegie's swimming pool has changed little since it was opened in 1905. The balconies with their iron railings still look down upon it and only the changing cubicles which used to line its sides have been replaced by more modern facilities. In this photograph there are only a couple of swimmers in the water, but many youngsters are seated at the far end of the baths and on the steps of the diving board waiting to take the plunge. The Dunfermline coat of arms is displayed on the gable wall above the pool.

4003. 20. *Interior of Turkish Baths, Dunfermline.*

Andrew Carnegie's decision to include Turkish baths in the new swimming pool building definitely added a very exotic touch when the premises were opened in 1905. Eastern-looking miniature palms decorated the wall cabinets and Turkish carpets covered the floor of this room, where users of the baths could read the latest newspapers as they relaxed in the welcome warmth. The baths are still operational and are a popular and well-used attraction.

To try to improve the health and fitness of schoolchildren throughout Scotland, Andrew Carnegie founded the Dunfermline College of Physical Education and Hygiene in 1905 with Miss Flora Ogston as its first principal. All of Scotland's women gym teachers were trained there until 1950, with the exception of the years of World War II when the students were evacuated to Aberdeen for safety. In 1950 the college returned to Aberdeen. It later transferred to Cramond Campus on the outskirts of Edinburgh and is now part of the Faculty of Education of the University of Edinburgh with modern premises in Holyrood Road. Its students are still referred to as 'Dunfers' after its

Dunfermline origins! One of the last students to complete her three-year teacher training course in Dunfermline recalls the strict discipline and emphasis on correct uniform that was meant to set an example to the pupils the students would go on to teach. In particular she mentions how progressive the college was considered for permitting its girls to discard heavy serge gym slips in favour of doing their exercises in the gymnasium shown here in open-necked white cotton blouses and navy PE knickers. She also recalls the many admiring glances they attracted from the town's young men, who seemed to find every opportunity to pass along the balconies seen on either side of this photograph while classes were in progress!

Andrew Carnegie's greatest gift to Dunfermline was undoubtedly Pittencrieff Glen. He stated that its purchase in 1902 from Colonel James Maitland Hunt gave him untold pleasure because it had been forbidden territory to him during his childhood years – a fact brought home to him forcibly as when its owners opened their grounds to the local populace for one day each year it was specifically with the exception of the Carnegies and the Morrisons, because of their radical political activities. Carnegie never forgot this deliberate humiliation which his family had suffered and when, as he had vowed, he at last became owner of the Glen he wrote, 'My new title beats all! I am laird of Pittencrieff, that's the Glen and Palace ruins at Dunfermline, the most sacred spot on earth. I would rather be Pittencrieff than King Edward by a long shot. I laugh at the importance of it. It really tickles me. But oh – those who have passed should be here to enjoy it. What it would have meant to my Grandfather, Father and Uncles.' The trees which Carnegie and his wife planted to mark the official handing over of Pittencrieff to the people of Dunfermline in 1903 still flourish in the grounds to the east of the bandstand as a living memorial to his great generosity. To ensure Pittencrieff Glen formed the finest public park in the country Carnegie engaged leading experts including the young Scottish town planner, Patrick Geddes, and internationally renowned landscape architect, Thomas Mawson. Geddes stressed that the park should be an integral part of the town, while at the same time offering its residents space for quiet rest and contemplation. This view shows the north-west entrance leading into the Glen from Pittencrieff Street. Mawson was particularly anxious that Pittencrieff House, which dated from 1610, should be preserved as the centrepiece. This was achieved, and between 1911 and 1913 architect Sir Robert Lorimer redesigned its two upper floors and opened up what had been bedrooms into two long galleries suitable for use as an art gallery and museum. They still serve this purpose today.

As well as the facilities offered by the tea house and its successor the pavilion (featured on pages 26 and 27), it has also always been possible for visitors to the Glen to enjoy an ice cream or cool refreshing drink purchased from one of the licensed vendors such as Vincenzo Macari, who, although his cart is still horse-drawn, advertises proudly in this picture that his ices are produced using newfangled electricity. His rival Georgio Pellegrini dispensed ices from a boat-shaped ice cream cart. On offer were penny cones, wafers and tuppeny nougat-coated sliders, which in those less politically correct times were known as a single darkie or a double darkie if both wafers were chocolate-coated at a cost of an extra penny. Both the Macari family and the Pellegrinis were of Italian origin, the latter running an ice cream parlour and fish and chip shop in Pittencrieff Street where their cafe also served as a tuck shop for pupils attending the nearby primary school. The addition of fish and chips to the menu of these popular Italian cafes was to ensure that they were kept equally busy during the cold winter months, although both ice cream and fish and chips proved equally popular with their Scottish customers all year round! Today, well-known Italian purveyors of ice cream and fish suppers include the Divito family with their premises at Crossgates and the Alari family in Chalmers Street.

While Geddes and Mawson provided many ideas for the redevelopment of Pittencrieff Glen as the perfect space for public relaxation – as Andrew Carnegie had desired – the actual work of converting it into the popular park which it has proved to be for a whole century was carried out by Messrs Backhouse of York, who laid out the paths, gardens and open spaces. James Whitten of Glasgow Botanic Gardens drew up plans for the conservatory, which with its coal-fired central heating enabled tropical flowers and plants to flourish in the cooler climes of Dunfermline. A more modern conservatory than the one pictured here is still a popular year-round attraction. The spire of Dunfermline Abbey rises in the background beyond the trees.

Equally popular over the years has been the tea house, the first version of which, with its verandah stretching the full length of its frontage, is shown here. The building in the background contained the old stables for Pittencrieff House and was later demolished to make way for the present formal Italian water garden. Many of the Glen's visitors came in large organised groups to enjoy school outings and Sunday school trips, the latter being a special feature of summer Saturday afternoons with their organised sports, but with time also always left to allow the youngsters to enjoy paddling in the children's pool. This still exists in front of Pittencrieff House, but is now never filled because of fears that water quality cannot be maintained to the required standards of purity.

The tea house, which was extended in 1907, is seen at its busiest on this Edwardian summer afternoon. The outside tables are fully occupied while children romp on the lawn in front of them, and a mother strolls past pushing her baby in its pram. The Glen's ever-hungry squirrels and strutting peacocks, both of which still delight visitors with their antics today, have always been a big attraction for both toddlers and older children. A pets corner has also long been an attraction, but it is currently threatened with closure as a result of protests by animal activists highlighting what they consider to be inadequate conditions for the animals and birds. It is not difficult to imagine what their reaction would have been to the golden eagle in its large cage, which in less politically-correct times was a feature which most visitors to the Glen made a special point of going to admire.

Enjoying morning coffee, lunch or afternoon tea at the Glen Pavilion is still a popular pastime in Dunfermline. The present attractively-designed tearooms with their art deco features and south-facing view, together with the adjoining music pavilion, were first opened in 1927 at a cost of approximately £5,000.

The rear of the Glen Pavilion was designed to incorporate the bandstand with open-air seating seen here. From the 1920s to the 1970s it was a popular venue for weekend and evening summer concerts. The bandstand is still intact but now sadly neglected, while the area where large audiences such as this one sat to enjoy music has equally sadly been turned into a car park.

Dunfermline Schoolchildren's Gala Day was started by the Carnegie Trust in 1904 within the grounds of Pittencrieff Glen, which had been officially opened the previous year and provided the ideal setting for the afternoon revels which followed the procession down the length of the High Street. Here pupils of McLean Primary School are marching behind their embroidered banner. Each school was either led by a local pipe band, as in this case, or by a brass band as in the other picture. The first gala was held on 10 June 1904 and the event is still an important annual occasion for the town's youngsters, although because of ever-growing numbers only those in the primary classes have been allowed to participate since 1958. A

second change is that since the mid-seventies, instead of being held on the traditional Friday in June it is now held on the Saturday to enable parent volunteers to supervise, instead of the teachers who formerly took part.

This second picture of the gala shows the pupils and teachers of Townhill Public School marching down the flag bedecked High Street behind their banner. The photograph gives a clear impression of the vast number of boys and girls who enjoyed taking part annually. Writing many years later, one of them recalled that: 'Gala day was the big day for us children. You should have seen us going to school that day, spotless, with our tinnie on a long white tape over our shoulder like a sash. Like the other boys I wore new grey trousers, a white shirt and socks and leather sandals. I always carried a flag, a Lion Rampant, which was waved at the slightest opportunity or even without any excuse. All of the schools had their set positions in the Glen which they occupied every year without fail so that parents knew exactly where to collect their offspring at the end of the proceedings. Once settled on the grass in the Glen, I have many happy memories of the teachers serving us with fresh milk which they poured into our tinnies and the luxury of being given slices of cake!'

Hip, hip hooray, the morn is Gala Day! If we don't get a holiday, we'll all run away! used to chant the Dunfermline boys and girls such as those seen here in Pittencrieff Glen watching the pageant which used to be a feature of the gala day proceedings. The characters on the horse-drawn cart represented famous figures from Dunfermline's colourful past, including King Malcolm Canmore and his second wife, Queen Margaret, who was responsible for converting the Scots to Roman Catholicism and as a result was later canonised as St Margaret. Prior to the procession all of the schools gathered at the Public Park on the east side of the town and then marched via East Port, High Street, Bridge Street, Chalmers Street and Pittencrieff Street to the north entrance of Pittencrieff Glen.

Andrew Carnegie always valued books and loved to recall that as early as 1808 his father Will had helped found Dunfermline's Tradesmen's Library. He was therefore especially proud of the huge number of public libraries which his bequests funded. The very first Carnegie library was, however, appropriately opened in Dunfermline. The fine three-storey stone building on the corner of Abbot Street and Guildhall Street is still a much-used and very valued resource in the town, with its spacious adult and children's lending and reference departments, newspaper and magazine reading room and local history room. The foundation stone was laid by Carnegie's mother in 1881 and the library was officially opened two years later by Liberal statesman and future Prime Minister, Lord Rosebery. A total of 2,811 Carnegie libraries were subsequently opened in countries around the world, and millions of users including the author will always be grateful to the Scottish benefactor who made it possible for them to study in quiet surroundings with rich reference resources readily available for consultation.

Andrew Carnegie's birthplace, the simple weaver's cottage in Moodie Street where the millionaire benefactor was born in 1835, is now a museum where appropriate tribute is paid to him. Around its walls is told the story of his Dunfermline family before they sailed across the Atlantic to start a new life in the USA in 1848. The main exhibit is a working Jacquard hand loom introduced in 1825 and similar to that used by Carnegie's father. Still in working order, it clacks into action on the first Friday of each month that the museum is open from April until October. It was the decline in the domestic textile industry which forced the Carnegies to emigrate and set up home in Allegheny near Pittsburgh where Andrew started work as a bobbin boy in a mill, ending his career as a multimillionaire steel magnate. Carnegie sold the United States Steel Corporation in 1901 and retired as the richest man in the world with a fortune worth $400 million. By the time of his death in 1919, he had already given away over $350 million and the memorial hall adjoining the cottage, which was endowed by his young wife Louise as a tribute to her husband, tells the story of his generous benefactions.

Happily for Dunfermline, Carnegie never forgot his home town. 'Lucky indeed the child who first sees the light of day in that romantic town,' he once wrote, and his gifts to it – from health clinics to sports facilities – undoubtedly made it a better place for them all to grow up. Carnegie's trusts and foundations in Britain, Europe and America still serve humanity today, distributing over $150 every minute. Dunfermline remains headquarters for his four independent British trusts, the Carnegie Dunfermline Trust, the Carnegie Hero Fund Trust, the Carnegie Trust for the Universities of Scotland and the Carnegie United Kingdom Trust. Heritage walks are held from the Carnegie Birthplace Museum every summer Sunday afternoon.

The Baldridgeburn Institute, which was opened in 1909 on the outskirts of Dunfermline, was yet another of Andrew Carnegie's gifts. He always remembered the working-class men and women from whom he was proud to be descended, and the institute provided local families with a hall and stage, meeting rooms, a well-stocked reading room with daily newspapers provided free of charge, and indoor sports facilities including a billiard hall. While Carnegie was sometimes criticised for being a hard master by his own workforce, he always showed great sympathy for the working-class families of Dunfermline and once boasted that he was 'brought up amidst Chartists and Republicans. Our family life is distinguished for having had an uncle in gaol in Chartists times.' The Chartists campaigned for six demands including the vote for all men and the right to trade union representation, all but one of which – for annually elected parliaments – were ultimately achieved. Along with most of the other Carnegie buildings in Dunfermline, the institute was requisitioned by the government in 1914 and occupied by soldiers throughout the First World War when Dunfermline became a garrison town.

The extent of Dunfermline's industrial prosperity in past decades is shown in this aerial photograph of its sprawling textile mills. It shows the St Margaret's Works owned by Hay & Robertson Ltd. Their premises fronted the appropriately named Mill Street and also ran the length of the adjoining Foundry Street. The railway line which ran from Dunfermline Upper station out past Oakley and on to Alloa and Stirling can be seen at the right of the picture.

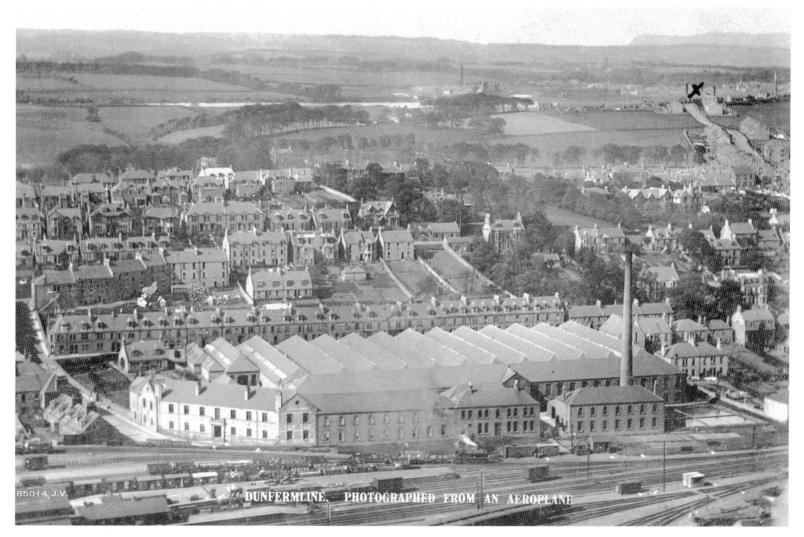

85014 J.V.

DUNFERMLINE. PHOTOGRAPHED FROM AN AEROPLANE

The Albany Works were owned by Walker Reid & Co. and ran along Gardeners Street. The railway sidings of Dunfermline Upper station are in the foreground, while Townhill power station is visible in the background.

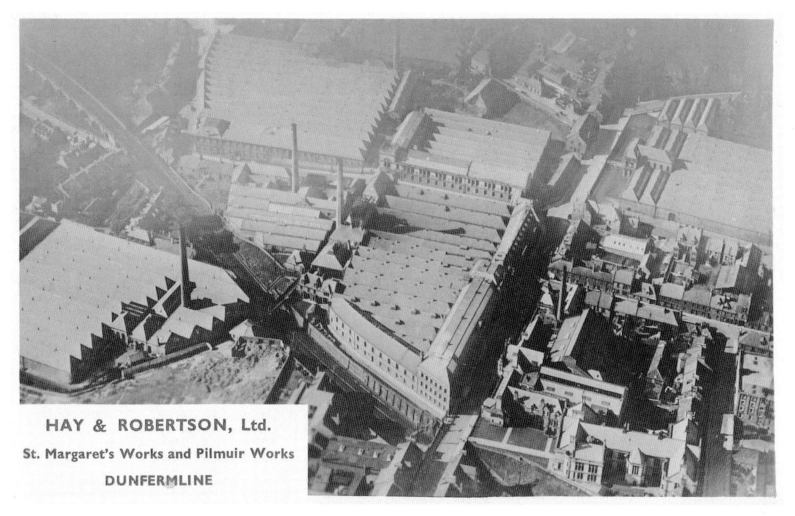

HAY & ROBERTSON, Ltd.

St. Margaret's Works and Pilmuir Works

DUNFERMLINE

This aerial view shows both Hay & Robertson's St Margaret's and Pilmuir Works. Dunfermline's fame for the production of linen damask was so great that its mills enjoyed the patronage of both King William IV and Queen Victoria, who as a young monarch in 1840 ordered items for her royal household. Her Majesty Queen Elizabeth II's wedding dress was made in 1947 in Dunfermline by Winterthur Silks Ltd. in their Canmore Works. Two of their employees were subsequently invited to the wedding celebrations in London. Dunfermline also presented other textile items as gifts to the royal couple.

The St Leonard's power loom factory, the entrance to which is shown here, was the largest factory in Dunfermline and the most extensive of its kind in Britain. In 1869 the works, which belonged to Messrs Erskine Beveridge, was described thus: 'Beautifully situated on the south side of the town, it is in every way a model establishment. Externally the place is unpretentious, but there is an air of tidiness and cleanliness. Many tons of yarns are kept in stock and given out in hanks to the winders, who by the use of simple but ingenious machines wind it on bobbins for the use of the warpers or on pirns for the weavers.' Linen production in Dunfermline ended in 1989. Earlier diversification into silk manufacturing had been undertaken by Swiss entrepreneurs at Castleblair Silk Mill, but like linen production this was also overtaken by the importing of cheaper synthetic fabrics. The building in the picture has been converted into spacious modern flats.

Gilbert Rae's Baldridge mineral water works were established in 1869. With branch factories in neighbouring Alloa and Falkirk, Rae's fleet of horse-drawn carts and later motorised vans distributed lemonade to families throughout Fife, Clackmannanshire and Stirlingshire. The company also sold a coffee and chicory extract for those who preferred a hot drink, and as the mixture cost considerably less than pure coffee there was a good market for it. Rae's was one of the first businesses in Dunfermline to install a telephone – all customers had to remember was the phone number 123, and they would be put through by the operator to the works office. Gilbert Rae was also one of the first in the town to own a motor car. It was a Daimler, and Rae ordered that it be supplied with two separate bodies, a wagonette in which he and his family could ride, and a second version with a small platform on which a crate of lemonade could be transported. This made it one of the earliest motor lorries in Scotland. Other Dunfermline lemonade manufacturers included Bissets, Danks, Douglas, Reids and Woodrows.

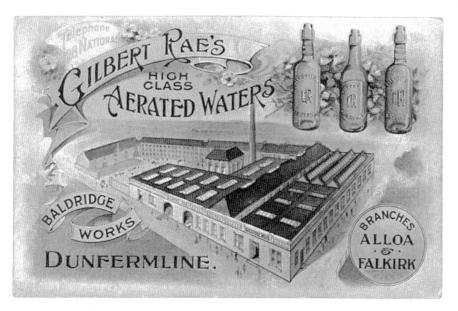

For those of Dunfermline's inhabitants who preferred something stronger than Gilbert Rae's lemonade, The Auld Grey Toon brand of whisky was marketed by Dunfermline Public House Society Ltd., an organisation run on the same principles as the Swedish Gothenburg system, which aimed at encouraging controlled consumption of alcohol among working class men, with the profits from what they spent being invested to help the local community with ventures such as paying for a district nurse. The reaction of the Kirk to this line-drawing of the Abbey being used to promote spirits is not noted!

DUNFERMLINE ABBEY AND PALACE RUINS

Dunfermline Abbey and the ruins of the town's former royal palace are seen here from the south at the start of the 1930s with a bus at the lower bus stance and only two motor cars in the car park. The Abbey was added to in the nineteenth century with the building of the Gothic revival church seen in this view. The new church enclosed the grave of King Robert the Bruce, whose tomb was unearthed in 1818, a discovery proudly recorded by wording incorporated in the parapet of the kirk tower. In addition to Robert I, it is claimed that no fewer than seven other kings, four queens, five princes and two princesses lie buried within the grounds of the Abbey. It was considered an especially holy resting place thanks to its close connections with St Margaret, who worked so tirelessly to ensure the establishment of the Roman Catholic Church throughout Scotland. Her shrine in Dunfermline attracted many religious devotees to the town over the centuries, and in 2000 there was a millennium pilgrimage to the shrine.

This photograph illustrates the thick stone walls of the Abbey Pends. Dunfermline Abbey was founded by the Benedictine Order and its monks conducted worship there daily until the Reformation in 1560. The adjoining royal palace, which was the home of King Malcolm Canmore and his Queen Margaret, was later given a new lease of life when King James VI of Scotland and I of England chose to gift it to his young bride, Anne of Denmark, when she arrived in this country to be his Queen.

QUEEN ANN'S CHURCH
DUNFERMLINE

The Revd Ralph Erskine was a minister of Dunfermline Abbey and a famous leader of the Scottish Secession Movement. This statue of him, with Bible open in his hand, still stands in front of what this picture postcard describes as Queen Anne's Church. Sadly it is no longer a place of worship and despite attempts to run it as both the Cafe Eglise and later as a children's indoor play centre, it is fast falling into disrepair. The building was originally home to members of the Queen Anne Street Burgher congregation. In 1942 a union was formed with the congregation of nearby Chalmers Street UF Church who had until that time followed in the 'Anti-Burgher' tradition of the Presbyterian Church. Further changes in patterns of Protestant worship in the town led to the building pictured here becoming known as St Andrew's Erskine Church in 1974. Since its closure the surrounding railings and pillars have been demolished to make way for a side entrance to the town's covered shopping centre, and this fine old church now stands disused and forlorn.

St Leonard's Church, on the south side of Dunfermline, has happily fared better than St Andrew's Erskine Church. Complete with its unusual round tower, it opened for worship on 17 September 1904 with the Revd Edward Houlston as its minister. It replaced what was known in Dunfermline as the Iron Kirk, a corrugated iron structure where members of the Brucefield Mission had worshipped as a temporary measure from 1895 – until completion of their fine new church – to cope with the increase in population in this part of the town. The church takes its name from the medieval hospital of St Leonard's, on the site of whose chapel it is believed to be sited. The nearby St Leonard's Primary School, built to cater for the children of the many workers at the St Leonard's Works, celebrated the centenary of its opening in January 2002 with the release of hundreds of red and

St Leonards Church Dunfermline

white balloons representing the school's colours, and many other events including an open day for former pupils. Current pupils were presented with medals struck specially to mark the 100th anniversary and a computer pen pal link was established with children at an elementary school in Saratoga, USA. This was to commemorate the fact that the decorative plasterwork interior of Dunfermline's former theatre, the Opera House, which was demolished to make way for the Kingsgate Shopping Precinct, has been carefully reassembled as the centrepiece of the Florida city's arts centre.

The staff of Dunfermline Cottage Hospital, which was opened on 30 August 1894 by former Provost Walls, pose here along with the fireman, Mr Robert Couper (who was responsible for looking after the hospital boilers etc.) and the smartly uniformed ambulance driver. The hospital's first matron was Miss Isabella Jack. The building cost £4,000 and an additional £3,000 which had been raised by private subscription was used to form an endowment fund. In 1898 the Moray Wing was added, with the Lauder Wing following in 1904.

A horse-drawn cart is seen delivering supplies to the Dunfermline and West Fife Hospital in this view taken by local photographer Christie. The hospital grew out of the town's original Cottage Hospital and in 1905 became known as the Dunfermline and West Fife General Hospital. It closed in 1993 when all services were transferred to the new Queen Margaret Hospital. Dunfermline also had an infectious diseases hospital at Milesmark.

During the First World War Scotland's only Royal Naval Dockyard was built on the southern outskirts of Dunfermline at Rosyth, on the shores of the River Forth to the west of North Queensferry. The dockyard's hurried construction led to an enormous growth in Dunfermline's population, and following the Armistice in November 1918 there was a huge reduction in work at the new naval base. A simultaneous increase in the rent of houses built to accommodate the incoming families and managed for the Admiralty by the Scottish National Housing Company culminated in the famous Rosyth rent strike. The strike, which began in May 1919, was well organised and by the end of the month a petition had attracted over 1,200 signatures. From the outset it was the women who took command and female street captains were appointed, carrying whistles which they blew whenever a rent collector entered any of the streets. Eventually 50 tenants were summoned to appear at the Sheriff Court. Irate protesters marched into the centre of Dunfermline where they are seen in this photograph at the ruins of the Abbey and former royal palace. There they were addressed by Sylvia Pankhurst, the daughter of the famous suffragette leader, who urged them to continue their defiance. The words on their protest banner read 'Rosyth Rent Strike, No Surrender, 50 per cent'. In the end, however, the tenants were threatened with a further increase and had to compromise that if it was not imposed they would pay up.

For many years the Dunfermline Highland Games was a very popular summer event held at the Race Park on Urquhart's Farm. As well as heavy events such as tossing the caber, the day's programme featured many other activities from pony trotting to wrestling, as seen in this picture. Throughout the day the large adjacent travelling funfair was a major attraction with roundabouts vying with side stalls for the crowd's patronage. One of the most popular rides was always the gallopers, seen below the striped awning in the centre of the picture. True to British tradition, although not the same in nearby continental countries, it can be seen that these ornately painted and decorated wooden horses were always mounted correctly from the left. Scotland's only museum dedicated to the country's travelling show people – whose names include the Cadonas, the Evans and the Taylors – is situated near Dunfermline at Burntisland. Ord Pinder's circus was also often an attraction when the shows visited both of the towns. Buffalo Bill's Wild West Show visited Dunfermline too.

Dunfermline's famous wee man, George Gibson, was sketched by local artist W. Thomson on a summer Saturday visit to the agricultural show. He was always smartly dressed in pinstripe trousers and cravat with a silk handkerchief sticking out of his jacket pocket. His lack of height was carefully emphasised in this line drawing by the inclusion of the bowler hatted passer-by in the background. Wee George seems to have come well prepared for his day out at the show, carrying what appears to be a plentiful packed lunch. A very popular local character, George died in 1899 aged 62.

The development of Rosyth Royal Naval Dockyard during the years of World War I resulted in many sailors in uniform being seen in the streets of Dunfermline. These ones were photographed walking down the New Row. The woman on the right walking towards the High Street is wearing a fur stole, which was a very fashionable accessory in the early twentieth century. James A. Kirkhope's photo studio is on the left.

Groups of sailors travelling to and from Rosyth are noticeable in this photograph of Dunfermline Lower station, which was built in 1890 ready for the opening of the Forth Railway Bridge. Unlike the old Upper station which opened in 1849 and was closed just over a century later, along with the line to Alloa and Stirling, the Lower station was modernised in 1973 and still serves the town today. Many Dunfermline and district commuters make use of the services to and from Edinburgh to avoid the traffic congestion on the Forth Road Bridge during morning and evening rush hours.

Locomotive 61101, a 5MT Class 4-6-0, gets up steam at Dunfermline Lower station. Dunfermline was the first town in Fife to be served by a passenger railway service when in 1834 one was introduced on the mineral line which connected the town to the harbour at Charlestown, from where travellers could board a ferry to cross the Forth. At its peak the Charlestown to Granton ferry carried 25,000 passengers a year, but as more modern steam vessels were introduced to the rival crossings at Queensferry and Burntisland numbers dropped and the train service to Dunfermline was withdrawn in 1863.

THE NEW GLEN BRIDGE, DUNFERMLINE

17

The new Glen Bridge was opened on 20 April 1932 by Provost T. Gorrie. It was built by Messrs Street & Co. using 320 tons of steel reinforcing and 6,430 tons of concrete, and took eighteen months to construct. Although trams were still running in Dunfermline at this time tracks were never laid across the new bridge, suggesting that it had already been recognised that their days were numbered and that they would soon be replaced by motor transport. This photograph was taken looking to the west, and the lack of traffic contrasts greatly with the busy stream of vehicles which pass across it nowadays.

Dunfermline policemen joined with the officers of the town's fire brigade for this photograph, taken by the local firm of Norval, in which the men are neatly framed by the extending ladders of their appliances. The town's former fire headquarters is seen in the background. This small brick building in Campbell Street was later replaced by the present much more impressive brigade headquarters in Carnegie Drive. This was designed by architect James Shearer and constructed by David Anderson & Co. Renovations in the 1980s cost £900,000.

This photograph of Dunfermline's postmen was taken in the yard behind the town's post office in 1909. Construction began in 1889 and the building opened on 24 November 1890. It still stands on the corner of Pilmuir Street and Queen Anne Street on the site of the original High School.

Forestairs once fronted the houses in the main street in the village of Masterton, on the eastern outskirts of Dunfermline. The gentleman standing on the right in the foreground was Mr Hunter who for many years ran the post office. Most of the old village was demolished to make way for the approach roads to the new Forth Road Bridge prior to its opening in September 1964.